spoke at RCPC event

D0840722

Psalms

Psalms

Joy Ladin

RESOURCE *Publications* • Eugene, Oregon

PSALMS

Resource Publications
An Imprint of Wipf and Stock Publishers
199 W. 8th Ave., Suite 3
Eugene, OR 97401

ISBN 13: 978-1-60899-349-9

For every you in whom I have seen You

God is making me now.

Nasia Benvenuto Ladin, 2009

Contents

Acknowledgement

Psalm III:6, "You're lost in me again," appeared in *Lilith*

Author's Note

I'VE ALWAYS envied the psalms of intimacy and anguish, in which the bitter flux of human existence is inextricably interwoven with God's loving, raging, transformational presence. In the lightning-shot space where Divine meets human, time shatters, splits, leaps like a river, and so does the soul of the speaker, now hunting God, now hunted, now languishing in despair, now reclining in quiet triumph against the pillars of Heaven. As I languished and triumphed my way through despairs of my own, I realized that I wanted, needed, to create a corollary to that psalm space, but a space narrowed, as my life had narrowed, to a single room in which God and I had no choice but to face each other. Angry, hopeless, desperately lonely, I thought of these psalms as a trap for the God who seemed to have left me behind, but as soon as I started to write them, I found God waiting for me inside.

God, it seems, had been waiting a long time.

Biblical Hebrew has no upper- or lower-case, no "thee" or "thou" or other dignifying signifiers to elevate the "you" of God above the human "you." Because ours is a culture that assumes God's distance as reflexively as the Hebrew psalmists assumed God's presence, I have broken with the English and American tradition of capitalizing the Divine "You" and followed the Hebrew convention.

ix

Since I capitalize the human "I," this reverses the usual typographical relationship between Divine and human. There are similar relational somersaults throughout the poems. In this too I'm following the Hebrew psalms, in which the tempestuous relationship between soul and God is figured as a whirlwind of pain and love.

Joy Ladin
Amherst, Massachusetts
December 2009

I

I make my bed in hell, and you are there . . .

Psalm 139

There's nothing here
That's not your fault, not bees'
Enslavement to nectar's labyrinths,

Not the cacophonous greens
Shaking themselves out like tangled hair, not
The sinking shiver of my blood

Or the phantom footsteps of disease
That haunt my spinal column
Searching for bits of self to seize

The way you seize on bits of self
You somehow lost
In me, not the terror

Stirring my depths
Like the sea monsters you created
When you were in the creation business,

Not the bombs
Your children strap on
To detonate in streets crowded

With children you seem, in a flash,
To have forgotten. No, I can't
Not blame you

For a single second
Of the light
That penetrates me non-consensually

Dawn after dawn, impregnating
With hope, desire, need
A body that couldn't care less

How far away you seem
Even when you are oppressively close,
Stuffing my nostrils

With blossoming breath,
Drowned hair dripping
Over my breasts,

Dripping fragrance, dripping smoke,
Dripping your most
Corrosive acid,

Possibility.

You scare me the way I scare the rabbit
In my path. I freeze,
Brown eye fixed on your approaching shadow.

Sometimes you rip me to shreds,
Sometimes squeeze
Till my ribs crack, always

You watch me bleed and blossom
Curiously, from a distance,
As though I were a furry blur of terror

Frozen between surrender
And the urge to disappear
Into the undergrowth

Of forever. You'll scare me
To one death or another
If you come closer.

You come closer.
I smell you on my clothes, my books,
The toys my children scatter,

My two or three private parts
Devoted solely
To radiating pain, my organs

Of need and pleasure. Why do you bother
To provoke this terror
In something small and unimportant

2

That asks nothing
But to be allowed to vanish?
Why do you bother with us at all

When your being is bounded
By no conditions
But absolute freedom

And absolute distance
From the bits of bone and truth
That come closer and closer to freezing

The closer we come
To you?

The footsteps of the Lord
In the garden. I know
The drill: I pull on my skin

And try to act human,
Knowing you've already noticed
The difference between the creature I am

And the creature you thought
You were breathing yourself into
On the sixth day, at evening. I know

You will clothe my nakedness, tender
But also disappointed
That I need to feel something

Other than naked
When nakedness is the image
In which I was created, the image

I see through your see-through robe
Of shy young stars
That sing very quietly

So as not to drown
Your image singing inside them.
You want me to see you

Picking your way
Through the garden of my body.
You try so hard

3

To be seen. I try so hard not to be
One of your hopes
Staring hungrily through the leaves.

I talk to you incessantly
But you can count on the fingers
Of the hand you don't have

The times I've heard you answer. Occasionally
I'm blinded
By your beauty. One blink

And the reassuring
Lids of life
Close over you again. Now

I have no life to lid
The terrifying continent of your longing
To meet a gaze

That meets your gaze
Naked and unashamed, an image of you
That can stand the sight

Of the image it was made in.

You want it both ways, to be the sun
And the clouds that smother it, the heart
And the heart that breaks it, meaningless suffering

And the truth
That redeems it. Nice work
If you can get it

But you won't get it
From me. You offer yourself
Like an apple reddening

Within my reach, dangling
On the lowest branch, a generous
Hermeneutical fragrance

Drenching every event, trivial and tragic,
In *eau d'significance*. After all,
What choice do I have? Your angels

Torched the trees
Of life and knowledge,
Although I've made a decent living

Battening
On their ashes. You too
Have a taste for ashes. Of ash. Of something

Burned a long time ago
And still burning
Somewhere close to my mouth, the smoke of you

4

Clogging my nostrils,
A cry for help
I've become too bored

To notice. You woo me with the fruit
Of your intimacy, infinity thick
As star-sparked honey, fine-toothed combs

Of forgiveness, the barely-remembered
Coo of a mother
Singing me to sleep on her shoulder,

My first bicycle, the welling sun-warmed
Strawberry juice
Of forever. You wash the dying

Off my hands
And stand there
With an indecipherable expression

As I die again. No wonder
I can't stand you. No wonder
I crave your presence, apple blazing

In the blazing crotch
Of history's burning branches.

Yes, it's true, I've lost
The world you gave me,
The blue and luminous world,

Round as a marble,
In which, if I squinted,
I could always see you

Shimmering in slow oxbows,
Mirroring the river's
Mallard iridescence, sketching your face

In castellated clouds
And sidewalk cracks
And the twitchy industry of ants'

Insatiable hunger to scour
Your every cleft and crevice.
The rain rained down pieces of you

That made everything whole
Even as you shattered, shining
Like a bandsaw, trembling

Like dew on blades of grass,
Fitting my nostrils to your nostrils, filling
My breath with your breath.

You don't want me
To forgive you. You dread the thought
That I might photosynthesize

6

The obsidian sunlight
Radiating from your skin. You can't bear
What might blossom

From the sickness-seeds you sowed
In the soil of my flesh,
Blackened shoots, like something charred

By forgiveness, the forgiveness
You can't bear
The earth of me to bear

When nothing made of earth
Is made to photosynthesize
The terrible spectrum of death and life

You radiate from your skin. You try to turn
From the shoots growing toward you
From the holes you opened

In the earth of this flesh
That receives your touch
As something that hurts

And hurts too much
To do anything
But forgive.

Joy comes in the morning
You say, as though you expect me
To believe you. You

Come in the morning,
It's morning and instead of joy
You come, and you expect

And I expect
And neither of us believes
We're anywhere close

To joy this morning. Even joy
Doesn't believe
We will ever come

To expect her. Every morning
Without joy you come
To tell me to expect

What doesn't, mourning with me every morning
As though you expect me
To start believing

Joy comes in the morning
Because every morning,
Unexpected and mourning,

You come.

So here we are, alone at last,
With only loneliness
Between us, roses of loneliness choking

Exhausted trellises
Of limbs and metaphysics, the overpowering
Fragrance of loneliness

Overpowering my resistance
To the slowly opening rose
Of your infinitely loving

Indifference—you call it holiness—
As you climb the tiny
Wounded trellis

Of my humanness.

Yes, I hear the question
In your voice, your voice
In the question that wrenches

My stars of pain
Into constellations, twins and serpents
And a woman who has no face

Staring in a mirror
At the emptiness
Between them. Yes, emptiness

Is my answer to your question,
A small, swept space
That neither storms nor aches, a little orphaned mouth

Whose lips are made of silence. Yes, I understand
Your silence in the face of a woman
You cannot face

Because you have erased her
Attempts to find some shape,
Some constellation,

In your glimmering syllables of pain
That seem to ask her
Nothing. Yes, I know that nothing

Is the only voice
In which you can speak without shattering,
Though as you can see

9

Something in me has already shattered,
Some piece of body in my soul, some
Metaphysical window

That kept you out
Or kept me in
Or kept up the distinction

Between your nearness beating
Like a heart
And the excruciating sky

Of your absence. Yes, I know your absence
Means you have come too close
For me to understand your question

Or distinguish you
From the stars of pain
You refuse to constellate

Into a sign of redemption.

You like to meet me here
In the badly-lit depths
Of Café Despair

Where none of your friends will see you
Ordering wine, squeezing my hand,
Coming on to yet another body

No one but you
Would dream of touching.
You think you might get lucky,

That I might let you in
For a glass of wine and a few sweet nothings
About how you've always loved me,

Might be desperate enough to surrender
The defenses I admit
Have never defended me from anything

But admitting
How much I need
The sleight of your hands

Burning in my darkness
Like the candles starring
The café atmosphere

That makes us intimates, intimating
Favors to be granted,
Though from your perspective

I'm already split
Into thighs
Of surrender and bitterness,

Already wondering in my emptied bed
If you were ever there,
Swollen with desire, and what

If any love you made
When you sowed
My void with fire.

Here at the bottom of Creation,
Soul peels off from flesh
And faces in your direction,

Toward the spiritual nuclear flash
That pins my shadow to the wall
In a grotesque posture of supplication.

Here at the bottom, I look at last
In your direction
And you at last look back, breaking me down

Into lusts and aggrandizements,
Ape cravings and reptile terrors
And single-celled desperation

To split into equal, identical halves
And swim in opposite directions. Here at the bottom,
You see with a certain satisfaction

That no part of me, at last, is human
But the part that's peeled off from my flesh
And stares in your direction

With terror and contempt
And the beginning of comprehension
Of how much I've cost you

And how little you stand to collect.
Here at the bottom, in the mud that glues
The slender bones of prayer

To the bigger bones
Of acts intended to grab your attention—martyrdoms and massacres,
Fabulous fasts, meditations so intense

They transform consciousness
Into a cloud shot with lightning hints
Of the face you reveal

Without special effects
Here at the bottom
Where flesh is flattened into a shadow

On the wall that represents
The mortal axioms—time, causality, difference—
That aren't axioms, here at the bottom,

But unfounded rumors
Of an existence that isn't,
Here at the bottom,

Where the soul that's all
That's left of my flesh
Presses the flesh

Of what's left of your love
To the shadow
Of my breast.

This morning we're quiet,
Sad maybe but quiet, weaned
From the dramatic breast of torment

That kept us tossing
Toward and away from each other all night,
Exposing our nakedness

As the covers we fought over in our sleep
Became smaller and smaller,
And maybe you hurt me badly, maybe you said

And failed to say
Words I can never forgive, maybe you left
Bruises on my breasts,

And maybe my love for you
Became a kind of hatred, my clinging
Narcissism, maybe I was sick

Of you and maybe you
Were responsible for my sickness
And maybe my sickness

Was a form of love
You had no choice but reject
For both our sakes, for the sake of what's left,

Lying quietly this morning, bruised and stripped,
Nursed
By the milk of aftermath, the sad but nourishing quiet

That flows from the breasts
Of longing and disappointment,
Your disappointment that my longing for you

Couldn't lead me to accept
The body you bestowed upon me like a kiss,
A hard kiss, a kiss with teeth and invading tongue

But a kiss nonetheless,
And my longing to disappoint
The presumption you call love

No matter what you do to me,
No matter what I've said,
We lie here in the quiet, soul to soul,

One an exploding universe,
One a sliver of glass,
Clinging to each other

In the physical silence
Of this narrow bed.

There's nothing here
That's not your fault, and nothing
I can't forgive, no injustice, no torment,

No shuddering glimpse
Of meaninglessness, not even the fact
That you gave me a heart

That can't refuse your advances
Without terminally blocking
The arteries of blossoming

Which is what you insist on doing
With the world you insist
On re-creating

Every time it collapses
Into the existential cursive
Of hope and despair,

Peaks cascading into abysses
That leap and soar
Toward your next

Unpronounceable vowel, the flux of being—
Do you know how much it hurts?—
Writing your name over and over,

A lesson I will never complete
Until I learn
To sound out your syllables in the dark,

A dirty trick, really,
That you created me to forgive
You as involuntarily

As my heart pumps blood
Through veins that are the branches
Of the tree of life you planted

In my decomposing flesh
While you cheat, abandon, bury your face
In eternity's ample cleavage,

And only now,
When I've given you up,
Fill my arms again.

II

... in the secret place ...

Psalm 91

I want to give you something
I need to give
But tonight I'm empty

Of raspberries, of sexual thoughts,
Of cruel things to say,
Of my children's faces, of love

And the memory of love, even love
As empty as a night like this
In which no sun will ever rise

Because there are no suns left, because the only sun
Is emptiness
I want to give you

Because emptiness is all I have,
A cup of emptiness,
No, not a cup, or the form of the cup—

There are no forms left—
A cup emptied of whatever makes a cup
Brimming with whatever emptiness is

When it's emptied of everything
But the need to give.

Seems like you've been gone for years.
I'm bored, irritated, flesh scratching soul
Like boiled wool, soul

Like a cloud made of lead
In a horizon that's fallen asleep and dreaming
It can't raise its head.

I lie in the dark, a bottle of wine
That might be vinegar
By the time you taste it,

Waiting for you to break me open
And take whatever's left,
My body, my fragrance, my chains

Of sugars and acids, my notes
Of half-remembered summers, oaks, vanillas,
Fingers of sunlight probing forests,

My finish that will linger
In your mouth
After you've drained my dregs.

2

Why did you marry
These hands and eyes
That can't understand

What they see or grasp, this hole
Where a womb should be, these blades
In my back

Twitching like unfledged wings
When I hear you moving in the leaves,
A furry, furious thing

Hunting and hunted
By creatures created
When you didn't know any better

Though you must have known better
When you created me, these lips
That now and then

Forget how to speak, open and close
Like the mouth of a fish
Drowning in air

It wasn't made to breathe
As I am drowning in you,
Acid ocean

Dissolving and enlarging me
With love
Of which I can't seem to get enough

To stop my head from spinning,

3

You let me pretend
You still see me as attractive,
Useful, a raindrop

Trickling toward drought-stricken roots, a hand
On the feverish forehead
Of some concept of justice

That makes you sick. You let me pretend
We can bring each other back
From the brink of death, but death

Is never where you stand,
So you, in your mercy,
Let me pretend

I'm a memory
It would sadden you to forget, a rumor
You neither confirm nor deny

Because that's the way
You keep me alive. To make
What you pretend is love

Both of us have to lie.

Here you are, under my tongue,
Like a wafer of the flesh
You don't know what it's like to have

Though now that doesn't matter, now
That you've lodged inside my mouth
Beneath the silent muscle

That for you is only one
Of innumerable tongues
All trying to kiss at once

The holes in existence
You, naïve and a little naughty, pretend to see
As gaping organs of love. They *are*

Exciting, those moments
When you seem to fill
Every hole at once

But now you are here, under my tongue,
Flesh of my flesh, blood of my blood,
Rustling quietly through my veins

As though you had nothing better to do
Than drain
And fill my heart.

You don't get why I beg you
To tie my hands to the bed
And stuff my mouth

6

With something warm and white
Ripped from the fabric of life
By fingers you tighten around my neck.

You think it has something to do with guilt and pleasure,
Or the origin of tragedy
In the human need

To act out what we suffer,
Or maybe the simple bitchiness
Of forcing you to savor

A capacity for pain
Almost as bottomless as your desire
To hear my cries

As pleasure. Omniscience
Oblivious
To the obvious: as long as I

Am free to flee, I can't fulfill your fantasy
Of making love
Out of mortal terror.

This morning I'm a fraying chair
You have no plans to sit in. What's left
Of a meal you don't remember.

This morning I can't remember
What we said to one another
That made me so eager

To be your place of rest
In the world you abandon
To create. This morning I'm no longer a place

You can abandon or create,
A floor and a ceiling
With nothing between them,

A tree that's fallen, silent
In the silence
That's all that's left to prove

You are still my forest.

Here you are again,
A breath of vastness
Leaking through the window

Your little brother Death,
He of the heavier breathing,
Left open so he could come and go

Though he knows it's you
I'm waiting for, the breath of you
That entered me once

And refused to leave
Until the mud I was
Learned to rhumba

Or at least to shudder
In your presence. To love you
Is to be afraid—I get that—

But I'm not afraid of your love
But of the chance
The mud I am

Will never inhale enough of you
To get the fuck up
And dance.

You're right—I should stop thinking
Because when I think
I can't understand

What we're doing together,
You with your blameless beauty
Thickening in my window

Terrible as an army
Called in to guard
Or pacify

A restive population—me—
Dying of—well, it's hard to say,
But certainly dying

Because that's the way you made me,
Built-in obsolescence
That can't stop complaining

Even when you are slipping
Through my window
In search of peace and quiet

And a warm, imperfect body
To ease the burden of the beauty
Of things that never die

Because that's the way you made them,
But you didn't make me
Not to think, and I can't think

Without thinking
About what we're doing together,
You with your undying beauty

And me with the ugliness
Of thoughts you think I shouldn't
Because then it will never make sense,

You being here, flooding my ugliness
With your beauty
As though beauty were some kind of justification

For the death
That if only I would stop thinking
Would start making sense.

We lie here listening to the rain.
I don't want to interrupt
The thunder and hush

Or move my head from your chest
Where your heart, honest to a fault,
Echoes what the rain is saying,

That I too am falling
Toward an end that will not diminish
The splendor of Creation

By a single drop. Rain
Is your equivalent of hope, hope
That isn't hope

For anything in particular
Because for you nothing
Is particular

And so is everything
And both are happening at once
In the soft grey shower

Of forever, a sermon
Your heart keeps repeating
Because it cannot explain

The hope you find in floods
That wash our worlds away.

You know I have no secrets from you
And though the opposite
Is far from true

I've learned to love your guardedness,
The way your tongue gets tied
When you try to talk about your job,

The way your eyes flash
When you realize
I have no idea what you're talking about,

That I will never do more
Than sit here open-mouthed
While you go on and on

Revealing yourself
To a creature who can't understand
And sometimes forgets

What understanding is,
Who asks you only the simplest questions
And pays no attention to the answers

You've given patiently, over and over,
Speaking slowly
As though teaching a foreign language

To someone who only reads lips,
Asking if I want truth or the lies
That are the only answers

You know I will accept.

How can I learn the song
The morning stars sing together
When death is condensing on the lawn

12

Of my soul whose night
Doesn't know how to end
The suffering

That is my proudest possession, a dunghill
With all the comforts of home,
Tenure and air conditioning

And all the bristling
Authenticity
Of a polyurethane Christmas tree

Bought to commemorate
Your swaddling
In the human shroud

Of innocence and agony
In a barn where animals like me
Chew phlegmatically

As incense burns and crepe-soled maternity angels
Wipe your milky lips
And no one's thinking about nails through palms

Or how you can abandon
Yourself so utterly
Without embittering

The song the stars
In their fading sing
As night is born into morning.

You turn out the lights, one by one, in rooms
I didn't know we had, rooms
Where, if I wasn't me

And you weren't you
And the place we share
Weren't the size of a postage stamp,

We could be having sex
Or something more intimate, a conversation
About headaches that won't stop

Or lives that won't start
Or the plans you have
For all those sparks

From all those shattered worlds
That never had a chance
To learn how lucky they were

To be created by you,
All those little fallen lights
You turn out one by one

In the echoing mansion
You build from our love
With room after room I'll never know

Because my spark
Of a heart is too full
Of shards of shattered worlds

13

To have room
For anything
But you.

This night is different
From all other nights
Because this night is you. You

Are the shadow
I have fallen into, the shadow of the planet
That keeps me rooted

With its spinning, the chime of tines
Of distant dinners, the close
Of shops and flowers at evening. Drops

Hang in the humid air of you
Bats swoop and stagger through.
Their blind hungers are yours, are you,

The night that makes this night
Different from any other
Because, no matter how hard I try,

I can't not find you.

Fireflies flicker
In the forest dark
Making light of their desperation,

Risking death
For what would be love
If love were the chemical reaction

Lighting their abdomens.
Cold light, crepuscular, shriven,
Just bright enough to see

How unforgivably
Beautiful you are,
Your forests and abdomens

And transubstantiation
Of your creatures' needs
Into illumination

You wear like a dress
So tight I gasp, a chemical reaction,
A burst of light

Just bright enough to show
I'm in love with you again.

for Nasia

16

You are making me now,
Right now, the clay of me
Warm in your hands,

The hands of me warmed
By your hands that shape them, shape a heart
That's never beaten, been beaten,

Skin that shivers in secret places,
Places that will never be touched
Except by the maker

Hunched patiently over
The stupidity of matter,
Leaving your mark between my eyes, my hips,

In the clay turning slowly in your hands,
Blinking a little in your light
As I learn to forget

The tenderness you reveal
In the act of making, to confuse
The feeling of your fingers

Moving inside me
With smaller, less luminous fingers
That will never reach as deep, whose love

Will never make me
Something that can think, can suffer,
As your love, finger by finger,

Is making me now.

III

... a weaned child at her mother's breast ...

Psalm 131

I don't, I say, know much about contentment,
But you shake your head and rest
A finger on my lips. You taste

Of oranges and rain
And nourishing liquids, warm milk
And hot tears,

And to show me the unimportance of contentment—
Yesterday it was happiness—
You crumble beneath my hands

Into stars without a sky,
Without any darkness
In which to shine

But mine.

1

I'm lost, lost in the beautiful world
You fashioned,
Sweet and swollen

With pain and pleasure, cumin and frankincense
Burning on some altar, orange afternoon moon
Smoldering between smoke-smudge birches

Gorgeously, senselessly symbolizing
Your gorgeous, senseless transformation
Of battered matter

Into beauty beyond comprehension,
Noises in my head, trembling in my limbs,
Spinning walls and trees

Whispering promises you've whispered, hissing
That you're still here, that the whirl
In which I feel so lost

Is the whorl of the finger
You offer me
Until I learn to see

Your face and live.

I'm not sure what you want me for,
But I'm sure you want me
To wait here quietly

Breaking down and breaking open
As days shorten
And the first trace of shame

Reddens the summer riot
Of you
Flapping and screaming, eating

And being eaten, flowing sluggishly
In rain-swollen streams
Choked by the limbs

You are always breaking,
Breaking and entering
To see if I'm still sleeping

Here, where you left me,
If I still want
What I wanted yesterday

Or if I've learned to want
Only what you give me:
The rustle of claws

In last year's leaves, the tensing
Of your invisible body
As you prepare to leap.

You teach me to speak, to say
"Thank you," "Go away," "alone"
And "never alone,"

"Both," "now" and "always,"
Little words like "death" and big words
Like "redemption"

Written on the leaves
Of the Tree of Life
Whose fruit—you teach me "fruit"—

Remains uneaten
Because I haven't learned to eat it.
I practice "day" every day; when you say "night"

I practice night, repeating each word
In front of the mirror, trying to curl
My lips and tongue like yours.

You give me verbs
To spin and shake and shape the world
But I'm too scared to say them

So I whisper syllables that rhyme
And make nothing happen.
This is human language, I whisper,

But you aren't listening. Your mind is elsewhere,
On the next lesson, the next word, the word
That will open every mouth

In gratitude and terror.

How can I explain
How much it hurts to be
When you are being

So terribly kind, comforting me
With cold and heat, moments and centuries,
The reassuring creak

Of the ceaseless wheels
Of blossom and blight,
The brainless brilliance

Of flowering trees, the feel of flour
Between my fingers,
The scent of my daughter's neck.

You're lost in me again.
I've grown too large, too hollow
For you to follow

The breadcrumbs of being you dropped
As you wandered the labyrinth
Of my body. Your voice echoes

From ceilings you can't reach
Because you are a child again, an unborn child
With no womb to curl in

And no way out
But crawling deeper in. At times like these
You regret the love

That lured you into the sticky mess
Of creation. And then, and only then,
You remember your wish

To understand
How the creatures you love so much
Could ever wonder where you are

When you are all around us.

6

You go away and I come back, I come back
And you leave, the shuttle
Of our loneliness and love

Weaving the oxymoronic child,
Eternally mortal, infinitesimally vast,
For whose sake

We stay together, a child,
Truth be told,
Neither of us understand

How to nourish or protect,
Comfort or discipline, fruit
Of your perfection

Bruised and sweetened
By human circumstance
Who wakes up sobbing

In the middle
Of the night, inhaling agony,
Exhaling paradise.

7

It's time the soul you planted in the soil
Of this unhappy body
Learned to love you

Without scratching, to recognize
And melt beneath
The kisses you disguise

As bitterness and licorice whips
And galaxies of glimmering suns
Dangling in drops

From dripping leaves. It's time for you
To plant me
Among your dripping leaves

And time for me to glimmer there
In ecstasy,
Time for you to make me

An instrument of your beauty
And time for me to play
The music of you

That can only be made
Of and through
The holes you make in me.

Like bath-oil beads
Your gorgeous hours
Slither through my fingers, releasing the fragranceless

9

Fragrance of your presence
Into the water of my being
Something that is always craving

You who are always dissolving
And always here, smelling
Of mown grass and burning leaves

And the octopus-musk of sex,
Your gorgeous hours
Trickling away between my thighs

Into the pool of always
I cannot see
Brimming between the saffron lips

Of your pouting lily.

You glimmer like dawn-threaded
Autumn mist
Haloing a strand of silk

Emerging from an ear
Of corn just picked
From a maze of tassels

Hushing each other
As you whisper
Past, leaving no print

In the damp autumn dirt
Of my flesh. For years you ripened,
Pruned and fed me

Sun and rain, waste, decomposition,
From seed to stalk
To something you could snap and strip

To swales of sorrow
Sweetened kernels,
Crisp and opalescent.

10

Your tidal tongue
Washes me, tendering
A taste of your love

To a creature made
Of dust and dream
Splashing in the shallows of time

While you smile nearby, high and dry,
Like a very old man
Watching a very young lover

Abandon herself
To an element he's forgotten.
I've always been naked

In your eyes. Always quivered
When your tongue-tip lit
On the hidden, fleshy nib

Of my desire to exist. Always known I'd dance
In the tide of your love
And realize

I've never left.

11

Come here, let me tell you
How beautiful you are, swathed
In stars and shadows,

How creation trembles
When you pass
Like wind through late summer grass

On a sun-baked prairie
You moisten like a tongue
Licking lips

Plumped by the collagen
Of all creation must forgive
To bring you

Close enough to kiss.

12

Your lips, twin earthquakes,
Tectonic contradictions,
Pause above mine, waiting for me

To complete
My disheveled human sentence, clauses splayed
Like wet black curls

Against the blank white forehead
Of death. Suddenly, I'm finished,
And nothing need be said

That isn't
As your earthquakes still
The quaking of my lips.

13